curious?about

LUNAR NEW YEAR

BY ERIN SILVER

AMICUS LEARNING

What are you

CHAPTER ONE

Happy Lunar New Year
PAGE
4

CHAPTER TWO

History of Lunar New Year
PAGE
10

curious about?

CHAPTER 3 THREE

Let's Celebrate!
PAGE 16

Stay Curious! Learn More . . . 22
Glossary 24
Index 24

Curious About is published by
Amicus Learning, an imprint of Amicus
P.O. Box 227, Mankato, MN 56002
www.amicuspublishing.us

Copyright © 2026 Amicus.
International copyright reserved in all countries.
No part of this book may be reproduced in any
form without written permission from the publisher.

Editor: Ana Brauer
Series Designer: Kathleen Petelinsek
Book Designer and Photo Researcher: Sara Hood

Library of Congress Cataloging-in-Publication Data
Names: Silver, Erin, 1980- author
Title: Curious about Lunar New Year / by Erin Silver.
Description: Mankato, MN : Amicus Learning, [2026] | Series: Curious about holidays | Includes bibliographical references and index. | Audience: Ages 6–9 | Audience: Grades 2–3 | Summary: "When is Lunar New Year celebrated? Learn about the history, significance, and celebrations of Lunar New Year in this question-and-answer book for elementary-aged readers. Includes table of contents, glossary, further resources, and index"— Provided by publisher.
Identifiers: LCCN 2025014072 (print) | LCCN 2025014073 (ebook) | ISBN 9798892008488 library binding | ISBN 9798892009140 paperback | ISBN 9798892009805 ebook
Subjects: LCSH: New Year—Juvenile literature
Classification: LCC GT4905 .S55 2026 (print) | LCC GT4905 (ebook) | DDC 394.2614—dc23/eng/20250518
LC record available at https://lccn.loc.gov/2025014072
LC ebook record available at https://lccn.loc.gov/2025014073

Photo Credits: Alamy Stock Photo/IMAGO/Xinhua, 10, michael mcleod, 17 (bottom); Freepik/mikibike, 20; Getty Images/Alexander Spatari, 2, 8–9, Bruce Yuanyue Bi, 21, Edwin Tan, 3, 17 (top), 19 (bottom), Hugo Amaral/SOPA Images, 7, Images by Tang Ming Tung, 4–5, Jordan Lye, 17 (second from top), Marcus Chung, 18 (top), Patrick Chu, 19 (top), twomeows, 11, whitebalance.space, 18 (bottom); MapSVG/unknown, 4; Shutterstock/dvoevnore, cover, 1, Hung Chung Chih, 17 (second from bottom), Roninjin, 15, Toa55, 16, 17 (middle), Tuleyhcm, 2, 12–13; The Noun Project/Brad, 15, DaeSung LEE, 15, DNY, 15, Fauzi Arts, 15, ghufronagustian, 22, 23, kareemov, 15, NHA, 15, PixelX, 15, Rank Sol, 15, Teuku Syahrizal, 22, 23, Vectors Market, 15; Vecteezy/Omprakash R, 4

Every effort has been made to contact copyright holders for material reproduced in this book. Any omissions will be rectified in subsequent printings if notice is given to the publisher.

Printed in United States of America

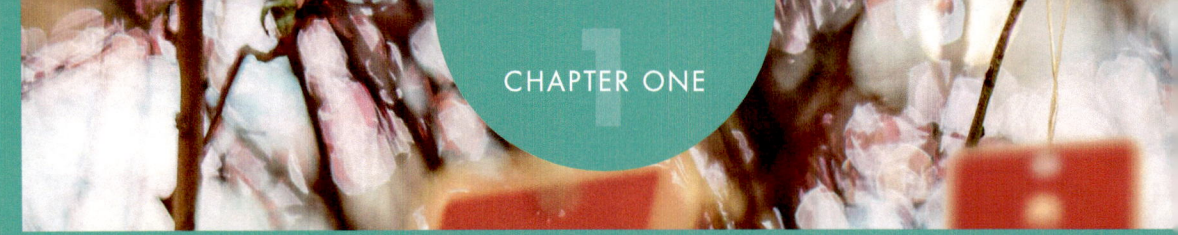

CHAPTER ONE
1

What is Lunar New Year?

DID YOU KNOW?
Asian communities all around the world celebrate Lunar New Year.

China
South Korea
New York
Vietnam
California
Singapore

Lunar New Year is the start of a new year in China. It welcomes spring. The holiday is also called Chinese New Year or the Spring Festival. It is the biggest holiday in China.

HAPPY LUNAR NEW YEAR

Many Asian families celebrate Lunar New Year with food and fun.

When is Lunar New Year?

It takes place every year between January 21 and February 20. Lunar New Year begins during the new moon. It ends at the next full moon. The holiday is based on the Chinese calendar.

Dragon dances are a fun part of Lunar New Year parades.

How long does Lunar New Year last?

People light red lanterns to bring hope for the new year.

It lasts for about 15 days. It starts with a midnight feast. It ends with a big parade called the **Lantern Festival**. In China, people take the first seven days of the holiday off work.

HISTORY OF LUNAR NEW YEAR

CHAPTER TWO

When did Lunar New Year first start?

Two boys' clay models show Nian, the monster in the Lunar New Year legend.

The holiday has been celebrated for more than 3,500 years. Nobody knows exactly how it began. But people believe in a story about a hungry beast named Nian. It attacked villagers in their homes and ate their food. Everyone was afraid.

Yusheng is a special Lunar New Year dish.

DID YOU KNOW?
Nian means "year" in Mandarin.

HISTORY OF LUNAR NEW YEAR

11

What did the villagers do?

HISTORY OF LUNAR NEW YEAR

Loud drums and lion dances help protect people from Nian.

The villagers decorated their homes and streets with red banners and lanterns. They drummed loudly. They also set off fireworks to scare away Nian and other evil spirits. On Lunar New Year, a special lion dance is performed with drums, cymbals, and a gong. This scares away Nian and brings good luck.

Why is each new year represented by an animal?

Long ago, China adopted a 12-year cycle called the **Chinese Zodiac** Calendar. A different animal represents each new year in the cycle. Every animal has its own personality traits, like bravery, honesty, and kindness. The animal predicts what kind of year is ahead.

WHAT'S YOUR SIGN?
Match your birth year to your Chinese Zodiac sign. Do you have anything in common with your animal?

HISTORY OF LUNAR NEW YEAR

CHAPTER THREE

How do people celebrate Lunar New Year?

LET'S CELEBRATE!

Red envelopes with money are given to wish happiness and wealth.

Children get red envelopes with money for good luck. Families meet and have feasts. At midnight, fireworks pop loudly to scare away evil spirits. The holiday ends with the Lantern Festival. There are dances and parades.

LUNAR NEW YEAR ACTIVITIES

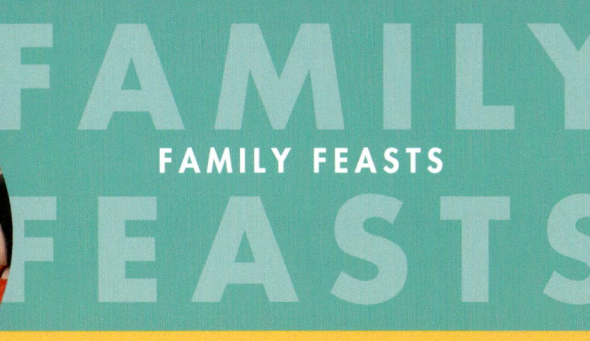

FAMILY FEASTS

FIREWORKS

LANTERN FESTIVAL

LION DANCES

PARADES

LET'S CELEBRATE!

People hang lanterns in their homes to celebrate the new year.

How do families prepare for the celebrations at home?

Red is a lucky color, so people wear red clothes for Lunar New Year.

Some families make their own decorations.

People clean their homes to get rid of bad luck. They also decorate their homes with red paper, lanterns, and banners. This brings good luck and fortune. They buy new clothes and shoes.

Families work together to set up for the celebration.

LET'S CELEBRATE!

What big celebrations happen in America?

In cities like San Francisco and Los Angeles, California, thousands of people visit Chinatown. They go to a parade and a lion dance. They also watch fireworks and enjoy festivals. In New York City, schools close on the first day of Lunar New Year. The city holds a special concert.

DID YOU KNOW?
Dumplings are a popular snack during Lunar New Year. They are a **symbol** of wealth.

Red lanterns hang across the streets in New York City to celebrate the holiday.

LET'S CELEBRATE!

STAY CURIOUS!

ASK MORE QUESTIONS

What foods do people eat to celebrate Lunar New Year?

Which American cities have the biggest Asian communities?

Try a BIG QUESTION: How do people in my own culture celebrate a new year?

SEARCH FOR ANSWERS

Search the library catalog or the Internet.
A librarian, teacher, or parent can help you.

Using Keywords
Find the looking glass.

Keywords are the most important words in your question.

If you want to know about:
- Lunar New Year foods, type: LUNAR NEW YEAR FOODS
- the population of Asian Americans, type: ASIAN AMERICAN POPULATION BY CITY

LEARN MORE

FIND GOOD SOURCES

Here are some good, safe sources you can use in your research. Your librarian can help you find more.

Books

The Big Book of Festivals
by Marita Bullock and Joan-Maree Hargreaves, 2021.

Lunar New Year
by Natasha Yim, 2024.

Internet Sites

Britannica Kids | Chinese New Year
https://kids.britannica.com/kids/article/Chinese-New-Year/390118
This site has information about Lunar New Year and its history.

National Geographic Kids | Chinese New Year Animals
https://kids.nationalgeographic.com/celebrations/article/which-chinese-new-year-animal-are-you-like
This site has information about Chinese zodiac signs. What animal are you?

Every effort has been made to ensure that these websites are appropriate for children. However, because of the nature of the Internet, it is impossible to guarantee that these sites will remain active indefinitely or that their contents will not be altered.

SHARE AND TAKE ACTION

Ask an adult to take you to watch a Lunar New Year parade.

Wish someone a happy new year by saying "Gung hay fat choy!"

Try a traditional Chinese food, like dumplings!

GLOSSARY

Chinese zodiac A 12-year cycle, with each year represented by an animal. Each animal has its own personality.

dumpling A small ball of dough wrapped around a filling that is usually boiled or fried.

Lantern Festival A big celebration that marks the end of Lunar New Year and the first full moon of the year.

Mandarin The official language in China and Taiwan.

symbol A sign, shape, or object that stands for something else.

INDEX

China, 5, 9, 14
clothing, 18, 19
dances, 7, 12, 13, 16, 20
dumplings, 20
drums, 12, 13
fireworks, 13, 16, 20
food, 5, 10, 11, 16, 20
good luck, 13, 16, 19
legends, 10
lanterns, 9, 13, 16, 18, 19, 21
Nian, 10, 11, 12, 13
parades, 7, 9, 16, 20
red envelopes, 16
zodiac, 14–15

About the Author

Erin Silver celebrates Jewish holidays, but she loves learning about celebrations all over the world. During Lunar New Year, she even slept with a red lucky money envelope under her pillow—then she got to write this book!